Italian Pasta Sauces –
Fresh & Simple

Daniel J Fernley

Fernley Publishing

Twitter: #fernleypublishi

Web: fernleypublishers.com

Copyright 2014   (6th Edition)

All rights reserved

Fresh and simple?

My father took me on a trip to Tuscany at the age of 15, after which I was hooked. The freshness and flavours of the sauces inspired me to learn more about this culture and the food. After much trial and error whilst living in Milan, I decide to put together some of my favourite recipes in this book.

The FRESH refers to the ingredients for the sauces. You must scour the shops to locate the best available. SIMPLE means I will not be stuffing complex pasta shapes. Most of the recipes you can knock up while your pasta is boiling.

We will be using dried pasta in the book. You can of course make fresh pasta very easily with good flour and fresh eggs, however at the end of a working day that is probably a bridge too far!

The book contains various images I shot, mostly in Italy. A few show the ingredients, but the book assumes you know how to soften an onion or deseed a chilli pepper.

Above all have fun and share with friends.

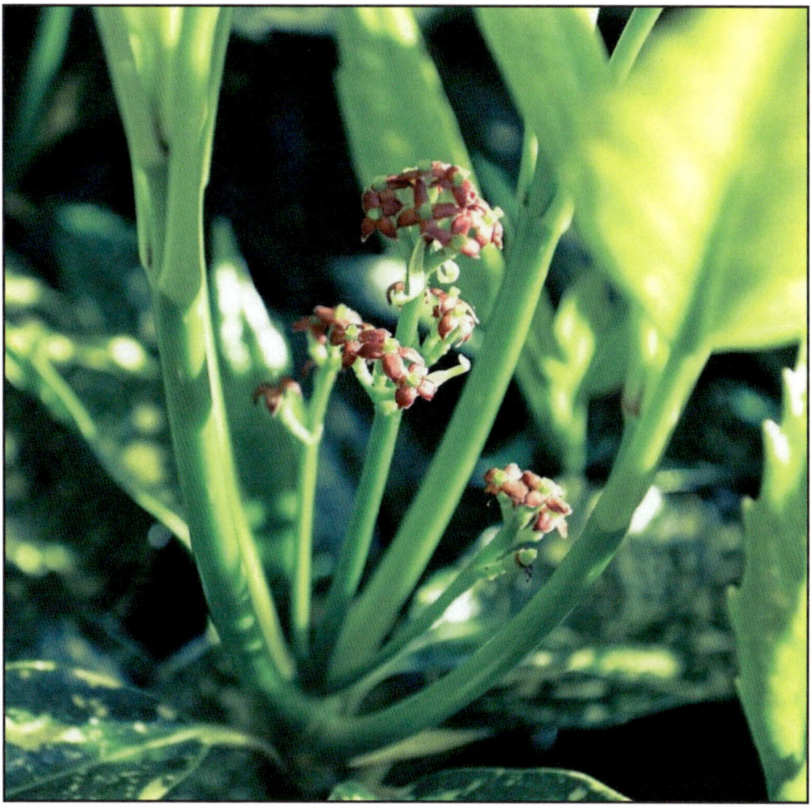

The Recipes

I am going to begin with some very quick and easy sauces, most requiring only a couple of key ingredients. You need to give them a try, refining to suit your palate – enjoy!

Aglio and Olio

Rosemary and tomatoes

Bacon & chives

Puttanesca

Porcini mushrooms with cream

Broccoli & Anchovies

Arrabbiata

Seafood spaghetti

Pesto

Clams & Tomatoes

Tuna & tomatoes

Ragu

Tomato

Cheese

Prawn & Chilli

Tuna & Capers

Scallops

Carbonara

Garlic & Parsley

Crab

Tomato sauce with fish

Amatriciana

Mussels & parsley

Dinner for two – Lithograph

Aglio & Olio

Olive oil

Garlic

1 or 2 chilli peppers

This is one of the most delicious and simple to make dishes in the book. Six or seven garlic cloves - peeled. Some fresh chillies, I usually slice a couple seeds removed.

1. Cook the pasta in plenty of water, spaghetti or linguine are my preferred choices.
2. Meanwhile gently fry the garlic and chillies in a good olive oil, but you must not burn them.
3. Remove from the oil and add the cooked linguine, stir gently then serve immediately.
4. Add lots of Parmesan and a good light white to drink, fresh salad on the side – nothing better.

Wonderful red chilli peppers

Rosemary and tomatoes

1 onion

A tin of tomatoes

Large quantity of chopped rosemary

Some parmesan cheese

Perhaps you have a small Rosemary bush in your garden, in which case this is so quick and simple.

1. Gently fry the onion in a little oil before adding the tomatoes.
2. Season then simmer gently for fifteen minutes.
3. Add the chopped rosemary and a handful of parmesan cheese, mix with some cooked pasta – quick & simple!

Castle ruins

Bacon & Chives

Some decent streaky bacon

Handful of chives

If there is a decent farmer's shop/market nearby, buy yourself some streaky bacon. Grab a bunch of chives from the garden, you can always use the green tops from spring onions if not in season. This can be prepared in the time it takes to boil your pasta – delicious.

1. While your pasta is cooking grill the bacon and chop.
2. Mix with the pasta and add with some butter and the chives.
3. Grate over some parmesan, a good grind of black pepper and serve – simple.

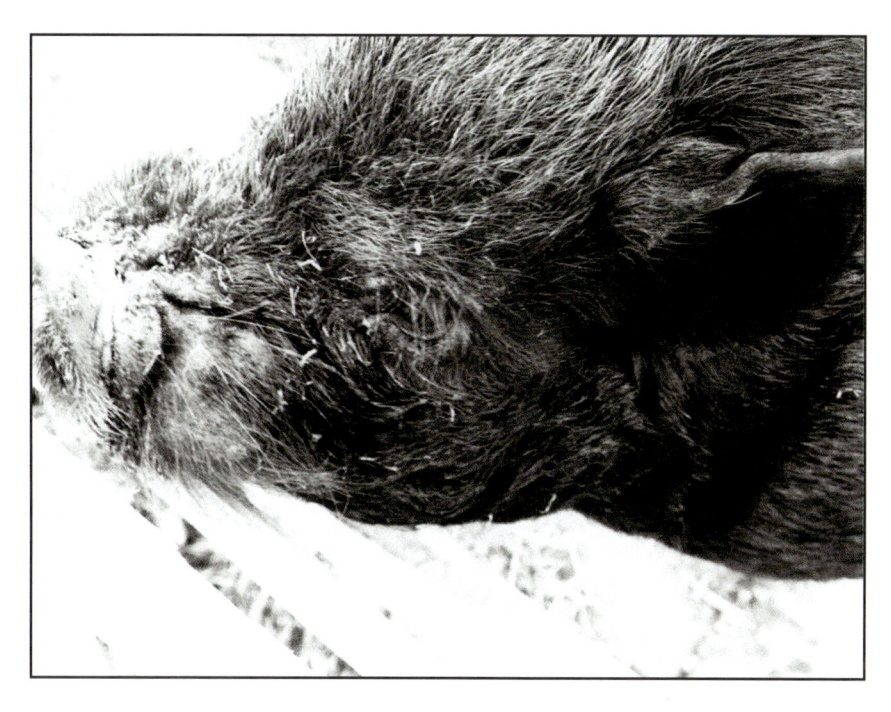

Wild boar in Sardinia

Puttanesca

Black olives

Three cloves of garlic

A tin of anchovies,

Tablespoon of capers

Fresh parsley

A tin of tomatoes

A feisty little dish, with bags of flavour perhaps with spaghetti, the parsley must be fresh.

1. Stone and halve the olives, you could buy them pre-done but the flavours are not quite as good.
2. Give the capers and anchovies a good rinse and halve the capers. Chop the parsley and finely slice the garlic.
3. Put a splash of olive oil and a knob of butter in a pan and add all your prepped ingredients. Hold back on the tomatoes at this stage.
4. Gently fry together, the smell should be amazing.

5. Meanwhile pop on a pan of water for the pasta.
6. When the anchovies have begun to melt together add the tomatoes and cook your pasta.
7. You could top with parmesan and/or a little parsley, but I prefer not to. I have also tasted this in a small trattoria in Milan with a few chillies in with the garlic, but it is far better without.

Il Duomo, Milano

Porcini mushrooms with cream

Dried porcini mushrooms

1 onion

Thick cream

Dried porcini mushrooms are available widely, you just need to re-hydrate with some warm water and then give this earthy sauce a try.

1. Soak the porcini mushrooms in a small amount of warm water for fifteen minutes.
2. Meanwhile gently cook the onion in some butter until soft.
3. Strain the mushrooms and chop, retaining the liquid.
4. Add the mushrooms to the onions and continue to cook. After a couple of minutes add the reserved liquid and cook your pasta.
5. Once the pasta is ready add the cream and check the seasoning. Serve with parmesan and a good Chianti.

Broccoli & Anchovies

Broccoli

Can of anchovies

3 garlic cloves

1 or 2 chilli peppers

Full of flavour with the chilli pepper and anchovies, I prefer this with my broccoli quite firm and some linguine.

1. In one pan cook the broccoli while in another gently fry the garlic, anchovies and sliced chilli in a good olive oil.
2. Once the broccoli is cooked drain then add to the anchovies and garlic.
3. Mix with the pasta of your choice, spaghetti works well.

Arrabbiata

Lardons

1 Chilli pepper & a garlic clove

A can of tomatoes

A wonderfully hot tomato based sauce.

- Heat the lardons, sliced chilli and garlic until soft then add the tomatoes; simmer while you cook some pasta – done.

No excuse for not making this yourself.

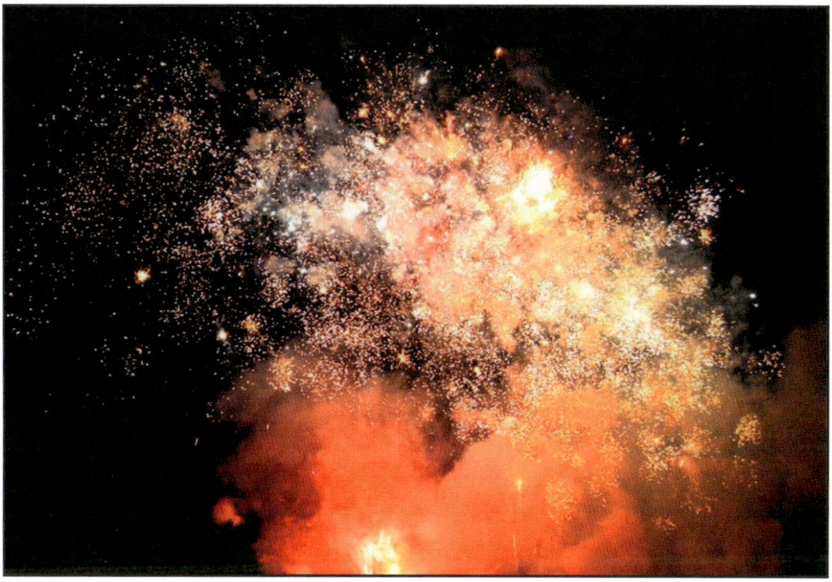

Seafood Spaghetti

An onion

Can of tomatoes

Chilli pepper

Lots of fresh parsley

Squid and some assorted seafood

This is a little more complex than some of the earlier recipes, but well worth the effort. You will need some squid for this one; I find an assorted bag of seafood works well as this usually contains the squid.

1. Fry the squid until it starts to colour then add a little white wine.
2. Allow to evaporate before you add the tomatoes and sliced chilli.
3. In another pan heat the onion until soft before adding the remaining seafood.
4. Add lots of chopped parsley to each pan then mix with the cooked spaghetti.

Notice how the door is enlarged to accommodate a barrel

Pesto

Pine nuts

Fresh Basil

3 garlic cloves

A good olive oil

You can buy some decent pre-prepared versions of this in good shops, but once you have made it yourself there is no turning back – it is like chalk & cheese!

1. Lightly heat the pine nuts in a thick based pan or in the oven.
2. Allow to cool then crush in a mortar with the garlic and basil. Use a little oil to loosen.
3. Add some parmesan cheese to the mixture and a little more oil until you have your desired consistency.
4. Toss with the cooked pasta of your choice and top with more parmesan – delicious.

I had a wonderful version of this in Genoa. As a slight twist they use a mixture of pecorino with the parmesan, see if your guests notice the change!

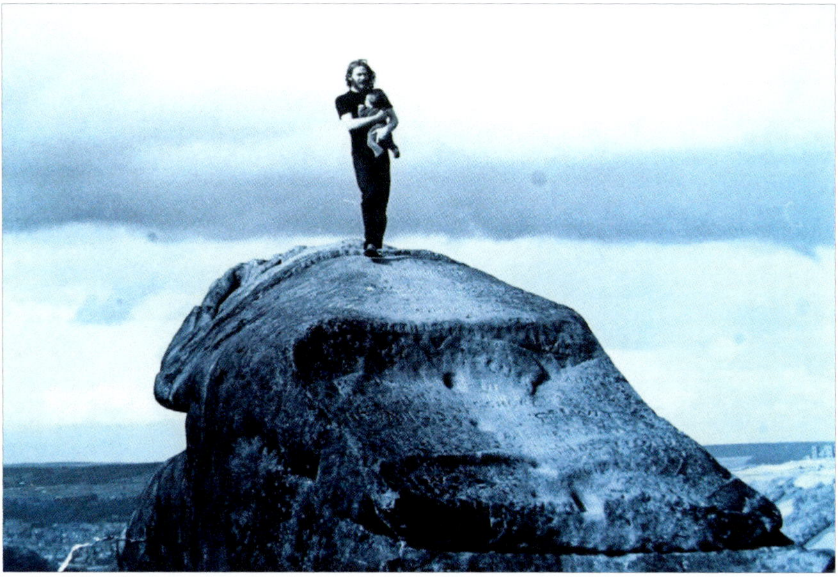

Clams & tomatoes

Fresh clams

Can of tomatoes

2 garlic cloves

Handful of parsley

A classic, I can remember eating this in a restaurant on the Cinque Terra.

1. I tend to cook the clams with a little water and the juice of a lemon. They should take between 5 and 10 minutes; discard any that did not open.
2. Finely chop the garlic and heat with a little oil until soft then add the tomatoes.
3. Cook for 10 to 15 minutes then add the clams and some chopped parsley – wonderful.
4. You can use some chopped chilli with the garlic if you want a little more kick, but I prefer it without.

Steps down to the Cinque Terre

Tuna & Tomatoes

A can of tuna

Some black olives

2 garlic cloves and an onion

Can of tomatoes

A very simple sauce using ingredients from the store cupboard.

1. Gently cook the chopped garlic and onions with the olives.
2. Add the tomatoes, season and simmer until reduced.
3. Finally add the tuna to warm through.

Colours of Italy

Ragu

Onion and a couple of carrots

Minced pork & beef

2 tins of tomatoes and some puree

Glass of wine

There are many versions of this, especially in England where we call it Bolognese! An Italian trattoria will make the real stuff with tomato paste and meat with a little wine, simple and delicious.

1. I usually go for a minced beef from the butchers rather the lean pack you find in supermarkets. Good to add some pork mince if available; you could just use a few good quality pork sausages and remove the skins.
2. Brown the meats and set-aside before gently frying the chopped onion and carrots. Add a glass of wine and return the meat to the pan. I tend to use a red wine but a good quality white works well. In cooking if you use a cheap wine then you get….
3. Add the tomatoes and simmer very gently for a couple of hours. Make sure you keep an eye on the mixture so as it does burn. Done.

La Casa di Arlecchino, San Giovanni Bianco. Perhaps pop in and visit the area if you are in Northern Italy.

Tomato sauce

Large onion

2 tins of tomatoes

A handful of fresh basil

Gently fry the onion in some olive oil until soft. Add the tomatoes and simmer. I often go to the local market towards the end of the day when they are throwing away the over ripe fruit, these are the best tomatoes to chop and add if available. We will stick with tins for the moment.

1. Cook your pasta and add the roughly ripped up the basil to the sauce.
2. Mix together and serve with a good parmesan cheese.

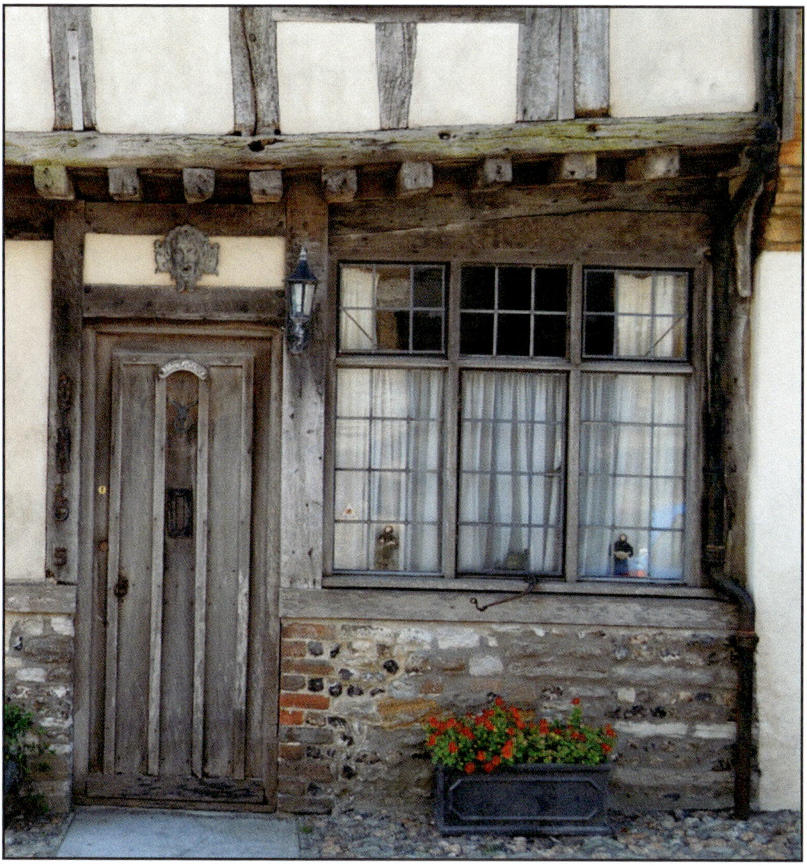

Cheese sauce

Parmesan

Emmental

Fontina cheese

Put a large pan of water on the boil while you grate some cheese you might have in the fridge. I tend to use parmesan, emmental and some fontina for this recipe however any good cheese will work. Once the pasta is cooked, drain but leave a little wet as it helps the cheese to mix better.

1. Toss in the cheese and add a good grate of fresh pepper, stir gently and serve.
2. Serve with a fresh green salad and a glass of chilled prosecco.

Dad and his beloved Alfa

Prawn & Chilli

Chilli flakes

Garlic

Prawns

Glass of white wine

Parsley

This is a very quick and simple dish. You can use cooked prawns, but better with some raw tiger prawns if available.

1. Finely chop the garlic and gently fry with the prawns until cooked.
2. Add a glass of white wine and a sprinkle of chilli flakes.
3. Chop the parsley and add to the sauce – serve.

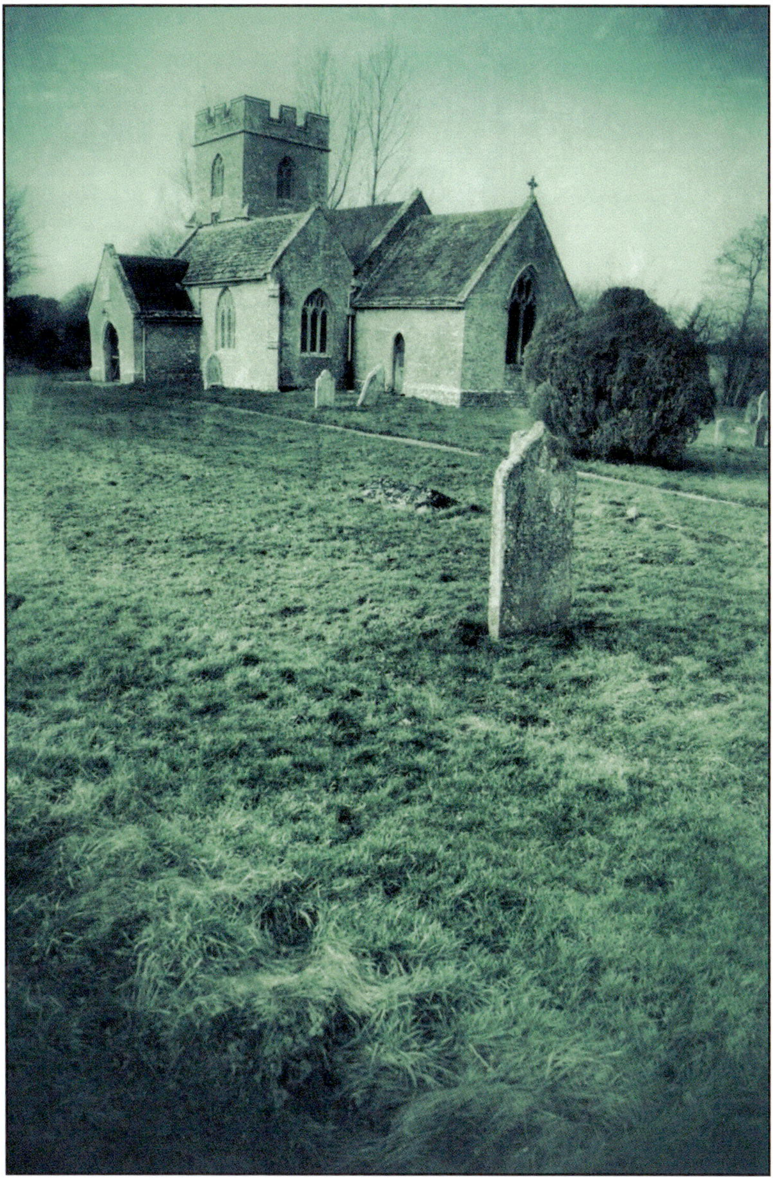

Tuna & Capers

Onion

Tablespoon of capers

2 garlic cloves

Parsley

Tinned tomatoes & tuna

This is one of those recipes that can be done from your store cupboard, just needs a large bunch of fresh parsley.

1. Chop the onion and garlic, fry gently before adding the capers and chopped parsley.
2. Stir in the tomatoes and simmer while you cook your pasta.
3. Finally add the tuna to warm through, season to taste and serve with your pasta.

Portofino – beautiful but the food can be a little hit and miss, as with all tourist locations

Carbonara

Bacon

Parmesan

2 eggs

Try to get yourself some decent air cured bacon if available, it will make all the difference.

1. Grill your bacon while the pasta is cooking.
2. Chop the bacon and add to the cooked pasta. Break in a egg or two, depending upon the amount of pasta you are making.
3. Add a good handful of parmesan and season with some fresh black pepper, mix well and serve.

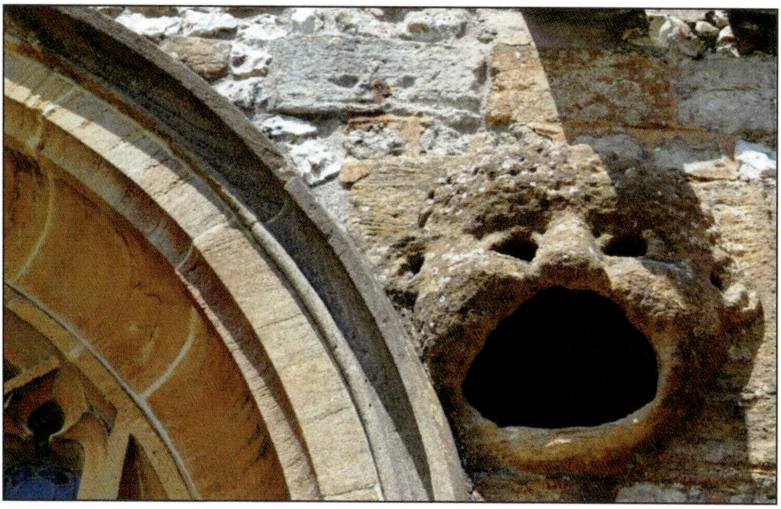

Scallops

Fresh scallops

Large lemon

Parsley

Quick tasty and delicious, be sure to smell your lemon!

1. Cook the pasta while you fry the scallops for a minute or two on each side.
2. Squeeze in the juice of the lemon and mix with the pasta.
3. Sprinkle over some chopped parsley and a good grind of black pepper.
4. Try this with a large glass of chilled white and some fresh green salad, simply dressed.

Lago di Como

Garlic & parsley

A large bunch of parsley

Couple of eggs

3 garlic cloves

Fresh pasta

This is quite a simple recipe but the addition of fresh pasta helps to elevate. If you have time have a go at making your own.

1. Finely slice the garlic and heat gently in some olive oil while your pasta cooks.
2. Separate the egg yolks and add to the cooked drained pasta with a good grate of parmesan.
3. Mix with the garlic flavoured olive oil and add the chopped parsley.

Quick simple delicious.

Milano

Crab

Crabmeat (as fresh as you can get hold of)

Fresh parsley

Glass of a good white wine

3 garlic cloves

1 or 2 chilli peppers

1. Gently heat the chopped garlic and chilli peppers while your pasta is cooking.
2. Add the wine and reduce slightly before adding the crabmeat to warm through.
3. Mix with the cooked pasta and chopped parsley.
4. Serve with a good grate of black pepper.

local publishing sign

Fish & tomato sauce

Organic onion or a couple of shallots

Tomatoes – tin or a good handful of ripe cherry tomatoes

White wine

Fish

For the fish you can use tuna or salmon from a tin if nothing else available. I prefer a smoked trout if you can manage to find some.

1. Gently heat the onion before adding the wine.
2. Reduce slightly then add the tomatoes.
3. Cover and simmer while you cook your pasta, add the fish to warm through and serve.
4. If using tuna black olives work very well with the dish.

Venezia

Amatriciana

Onion

Pancetta or a good streaky bacon.

Tomatoes – tinned or very ripe fresh ones

Red wine – a good chianti if available

1 or 2 chilli peppers

You can use 1 or 2 chillies depending upon how hot you like your sauce.

1. Gently heat the chopped onion, chilli and pancetta in some oil until soft, then add some wine and reduce before adding the tomatoes.
2. Simmer while you cook your pasta, I find linguine or bucatini works well with this sauce.

Vernazza, Cinque Terre

Mussels & Parsley

Mussels (and prawns if available)

White wine

Lemon

Good handful of parsley

3 garlic cloves

1 or 2 chilli peppers

1. Clean the mussels in cold water, discarding any that are open.
2. Gently fry the garlic and chilli until soft, before adding the wine and mussels.
3. Cover with a lid for a couple of minutes until the mussels have opened. If using prawns add until cooked, chopped parsley and a good squeeze of lemon.
4. Season well and serve with cooked spaghetti – wonderful.

Looking for mushrooms in the woods

INDEX

Aglio and Olio	10
Amatriciana	52
Arrabbiata	22
Bacon & chives	14
Broccoli & Anchovies	20
Carbonara	42
Cheese	36
Clams & Tomatoes	28
Crab	48
Garlic & Parsley	45
Mussels & parsley	54
Pesto	26

Porcini mushrooms with cream	18
Prawn & Chilli	38
Puttanesca	16
Ragu	32
Seafood spaghetti	24
Tomato	34
Tomato sauce with fish	50
Tuna & Capers	40
Tuna & tomatoes	30
Rosemary and tomatoes	12
Scallops	44

Made in the USA
Charleston, SC
18 December 2014